第一本图画词典
动物

First Picture Dictionary
Animals

猪 Pig

兔子 Rabbit

蝴蝶 Butterfly

狐狸 Fox

插画：安娜·伊瓦尼尔

www.kidkiddos.com
Copyright ©2024 by KidKiddos Books Ltd.
support@kidkiddos.com

All rights reserved. No part of this book may be reproduced in any form or by any electronic or mechanical means, including information storage and retrieval systems, without written permission from the publisher, except in the case of a reviewer, who may quote brief passages embodied in critical articles or in a review.
First edition, 2025

Library and Archives Canada Cataloguing in Publication
First Picture Dictionary – Animals (Simplified Chinese English Bilingual edition)
ISBN: 978-1-83416-417-5 paperback
ISBN: 978-1-83416-418-2 hardcover
ISBN: 978-1-83416-416-8 eBook

野生动物
Wild Animals

狮子
Lion

老虎
Tiger

长颈鹿
Giraffe

✦长颈鹿是陆地上最高的动物。
✦*A giraffe is the tallest animal on land.*

大象
Elephant

猴子
Monkey

野生动物
Wild Animals

河马
Hippopotamus

熊猫
Panda

狐狸
Fox

犀牛
Rhino

鹿
Deer

驼鹿
Moose

狼
Wolf

✦驼鹿是优秀的游泳者，还能潜入水中吃植物！

✦*A moose is a great swimmer and can dive underwater to eat plants!*

松鼠
Squirrel

树袋熊
Koala

✦松鼠会把坚果藏起来过冬，但有时会忘记藏在哪儿了！

✦*A squirrel hides nuts for winter, but sometimes forgets where it put them!*

大猩猩
Gorilla

宠物
Pets

金丝雀
Canary

✦青蛙不仅用肺呼吸,还能通过皮肤呼吸!
✦*A frog can breathe through its skin as well as its lungs!*

豚鼠
Guinea Pig

青蛙
Frog

仓鼠
Hamster

金鱼
Goldfish

狗
Dog

✦有些鹦鹉会模仿说话，甚至像人一样笑！
✦*Some parrots can copy words and even laugh like a human!*

猫
Cat

鹦鹉
Parrot

农场里的动物
Animals at the Farm

牛
Cow

鸡
Chicken

鸭子
Duck

绵羊
Sheep

马
Horse

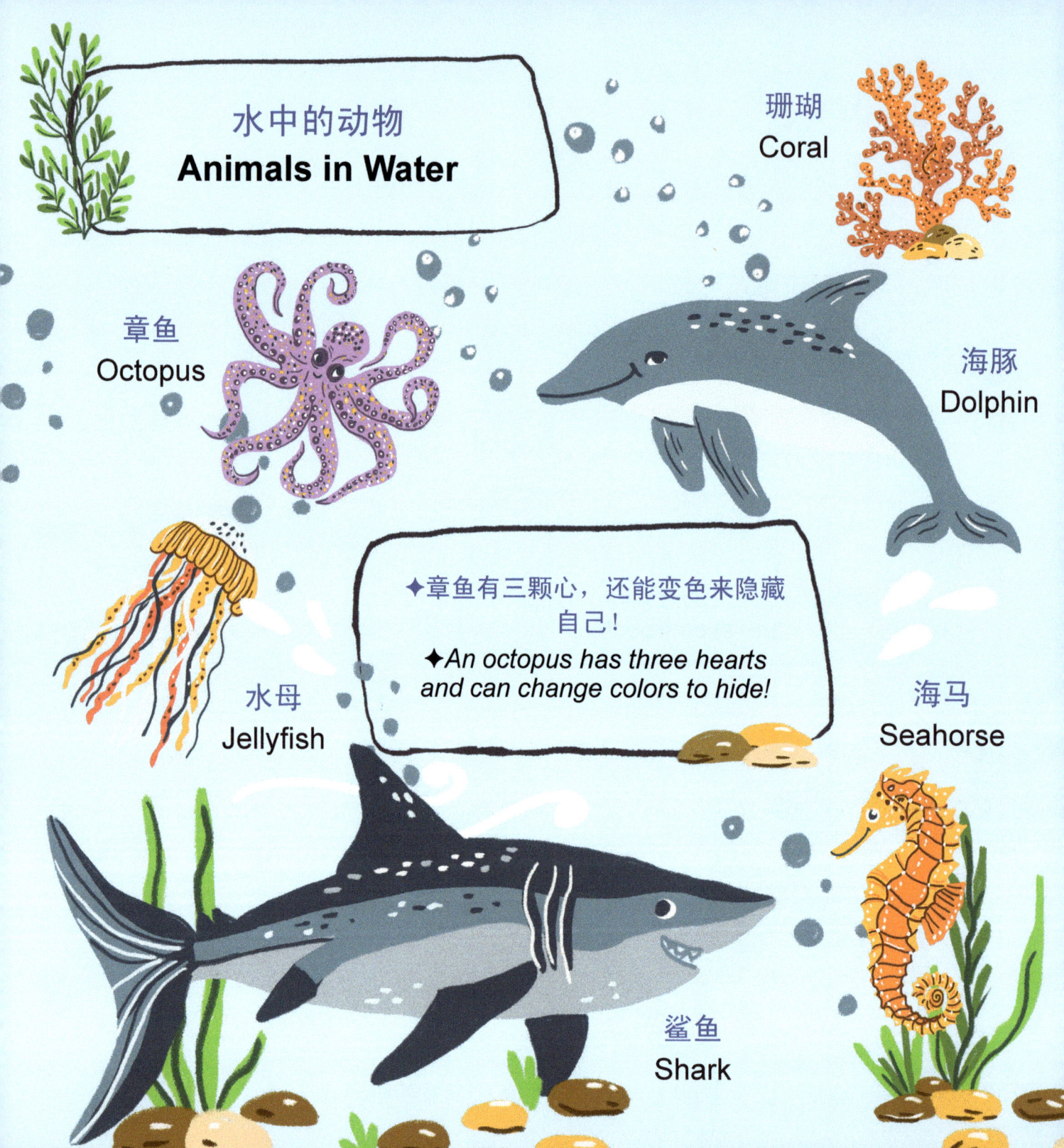

蚊子
Mosquito

蜻蜓
Dragonfly

> ◆蜻蜓是地球上最早出现的昆虫之一，比恐龙还早！
> ◆*A dragonfly was one of the first insects on Earth, even before dinosaurs!*

蜜蜂
Bee

蝴蝶
Butterfly

瓢虫
Ladybug

小型动物
Small Animals

变色龙
Chameleon

蜘蛛
Spider

✦鸵鸟是最大的鸟类，但它却不会飞！
✦*An ostrich is the biggest bird, but it cannot fly!*

蜜蜂
Bee

✦蜗牛把它的家驮在自己背上，移动的非常缓慢。
✦*A snail carries its home on its back and moves very slowly.*

蜗牛
Snail

老鼠
Mouse

安静的动物
Quiet Animals

瓢虫
Ladybug

乌龟
Turtle

✦ 乌龟既能在陆地上生活，也能在水中生活。
✦ A turtle can live both on land and in water.

鱼
Fish

蜥蜴
Lizard

猫头鹰
Owl

蝙蝠
Bat

✦萤火虫在夜间发光，是为了找到其他萤火虫。
✦*A firefly glows at night to find other fireflies.*

✦猫头鹰在夜间捕猎，用听觉来寻找食物！
✦*An owl hunts at night and uses its hearing to find food!*

浣熊
Raccoon

食鸟蛛
Tarantula

色彩缤纷的动物们
Colorful Animals

火烈鸟是粉红色的
A flamingo is pink

猫头鹰是棕色的
An owl is brown

天鹅是白色的
A swan is white

章鱼是紫色的
An octopus is purple

青蛙是绿色的
A frog is green

- 青蛙是绿色的，所以它可以藏在树叶中。
- *A frog is green, so it can hide among the leaves.*

动物和它们的宝宝
Animals and Their Babies

母牛和小牛
Cow and Calf

猫和小猫
Cat and Kitten

母鸡和小鸡
Chicken and Chick

✦小鸡在孵化前就能和妈妈"说话"。
✦*A chick talks to its mother even before it hatches.*

狗和小狗
Dog and Puppy

蝴蝶和毛毛虫
Butterfly and Caterpillar

绵羊和小羊
Sheep and Lamb

马和小马
Horse and Foal

猪和小猪
Pig and Piglet

山羊和小羊
Goat and Kid

www.ingramcontent.com/pod-product-compliance
Lightning Source LLC
LaVergne TN
LVHW072001060526
838200LV00010B/254